Genre Biography

MW00570687

Essential Question
What can people do to bring about a positive change?

Jane Addams
A Woman of Action
by Jane Buxton

PEACE

Chapter 1

Early Years

Have you ever wondered what to do with your life? Jane Addams spent a long time figuring out what her life's work was going to be.

Jane was born in 1860 and grew up as the youngest child in a wealthy family in the small town of Cedarville, Illinois. Her mother died when Jane was only two and a half years old, so Jane was raised by her father, older sisters, and later, her step-mother. Jane's father, John Addams, owned several businesses and was involved in politics. He was a state senator from 1854 to 1870. Mr. Addams was also a **philanthropist**, a person who does charitable things for others.

Even as a young girl, Jane wanted to make a difference in the world.

Jane adored her father and she **emulated** him in many ways. Under his influence, she grew up to be tolerant and kindhearted, and she inherited his love of books and learning.

Her kindheartedness meant that even as a girl, Jane observed that people often lived unequal lives. She could not understand why some people lived in big homes in one neighborhood, while at the same time, other people lived in much smaller houses in another. Jane decided that one day she would live in a big house surrounded by smaller houses.

Jane's father, John Huy Addams, was a successful landowner, miller, and banker.

Jane knew she wanted to spend her life helping the poor, so she decided to become a doctor. Jane's father did not support her plan. He wanted Jane to get married and have a family because that was what young women of the time were expected to do. Jane wasn't interested in marriage, but she also didn't want to defy her father.

Although she didn't study medicine, Addams still had a good education. She studied at Rockford Female Seminary from 1877 to 1881, where she excelled in reading, writing, and public speaking. These were skills that would be very useful to Addams later on. She was also class president for four years and editor of the school magazine.

Addams (holding the parasol) enjoyed Rockford Female Seminary and made some good friends while she was there.

When Addams was 21 years old, her father died. She was devastated. She enrolled at the Women's Medical College in Philadelphia, but she was so depressed by her father's death that she was unable to concentrate on her studies. Addams had tuberculosis as a child, which left her with a curve in her spine. This made it painful for her to study for long hours. And then Addams became ill. She gave up college and her dream of becoming a doctor.

From 1883 to 1885, Addams traveled overseas. She went to London, where she witnessed terrible poverty. She wished she could find a way to help, but what could she do? She knew she wanted to make some kind of positive change for those living in poverty, but she didn't know how.

In 1887, Addams returned to England. This time, she visited a settlement house called Toynbee Hall in a poor section of London. Toynbee Hall was an experiment by a group of well-educated young men whose goal was to improve the lives of poor people. It was called a settlement house because the young men settled there to live. While they lived among the local people, they offered classes in singing, reading, and drawing.

Addams was excited because at last she had a plan. She would establish a settlement house back home.

Extreme Poverty

Addams visited a market in London. It was the end of the week, and the market was closing. Cartloads of old, leftover meat, fruit, and vegetables were being sold inexpensively. The food was already rotten, but thin, sickly pale people dressed in rags were desperately reaching for it. Jane never forgot what she saw. She wrote later of seeing "hands, empty, pathetic, nerveless and workworn ... clutching forward for food which was already unfit to eat."

Chapter 2

Addams Takes Action

Addams returned to Illinois, and with her friend, Ellen Starr, began to search for a house to rent. They found an old, dilapidated mansion, Hull House, in the middle of a poor area of Chicago where many immigrants had settled.

Hull House had once been surrounded by **expansive** grounds, but over the years the land had been sold and many smaller houses had sprung up all around it. Addams's childhood decision to live in a big house surrounded by smaller ones was finally taking shape. The two friends decided to model their house on Toynbee Hall.

Wealthy, educated Americans were often shocked when they heard about the extreme **economic gap** between rich and poor people. Addams and Starr decided that Hull House would have two purposes. One purpose would be to provide a way for wealthy people to learn about poor people as the wealthy worked to improve the lives of the poor.

Hull House was originally owned by a wealthy businessman, Charles Hull. The mansion had been built in 1856.

The other purpose was to offer the local people opportunities, such as education and music lessons, that were usually reserved for the wealthy.

Addams and Starr wanted well-educated women and men to come to live at Hull House. While they lived there, they would get to know the people in the poor, rundown houses in the neighborhood. They would also organize lectures, clubs, and classes for their less fortunate neighbors.

Addams had enough money of her own to repair Hull House and fill it with furniture, but she also sought money from other wealthy citizens to help keep the house running.

Life in the City

Industry was booming in Chicago at the time that Addams and Starr set up Hull House. Thousands of immigrants from Europe had flocked to America hoping for a better way of life. Many immigrants had come to Chicago to look for work in factories, but then they struggled to learn English and earn enough money to survive. Often, men, women, and children worked long hours in poor conditions for very little pay, while their bosses, the business owners, became extremely wealthy.

With great anticipation, Addams and Starr opened Hull House in 1889. Other well-educated people were eager to help, and they came to live at Hull House, too. Addams relied on the help of these volunteers to run Hull House and the programs they offered.

The house became a popular meeting place for the local people. Hull House offered classes on many subjects, including English for immigrants. Eventually, it housed a theater, a library, an art gallery, a kitchen, a gymnasium, and a music school. It also provided many services that the local people couldn't otherwise afford, such as child care, medical care, and legal aid.

Thousands of people visited Hull House and couldn't help but be impressed by what they saw there.

Addams started clubs for children.

Valuing Traditions

Addams set up a labor museum at Hull House as a way to show that older immigrants were valued. They used old spinning frames and weaving looms to demonstrate their knowledge of traditional arts and crafts to younger members of the community. Addams said of the museum, that "far beyond its direct educational value, we prize it because it so often puts the immigrants into the position of teachers, ... it affords them a pleasant change from the tutelage in which all Americans, including their own children, are so apt to hold them."

Addams became known as a kind, compassionate person who was an outspoken **advocate** for the poor. She gave talks to many different groups and organizations, spreading the word about helping the poor. Addams became famous throughout the United States, and as a result of her work, many other settlement houses were created in other cities. Hull House was a model for helping the less fortunate.

However, Hull House needed money to keep going. Addams began writing books. She was a good writer, and her autobiography, *Twenty Years at Hull House*, became very famous. Addams made a great deal of money from her books. She poured the profits from her writing back into her work at Hull House.

Addams wrote a total of 13 books.

Chapter 3

Changing the World

In Addams's lifetime, women, men, and children from the poor areas of Chicago all worked outside the home. Even children held full-time jobs. Most worked long hours for very little pay, and they were expected to work in terrible conditions. However, they needed the money and would starve if they didn't work.

Addams heard of three children who were injured at the factory where they worked. One of them died. The machine they had used was hazardous, so Addams talked to the factory owner and asked him to put a protective cage over the dangerous machine. She was shocked when the owner refused to do anything that would protect the children.

Children often worked long hours in textile mills.

Children Are Cheap

Most factory bosses did not want the child labor laws to be changed. They argued that child labor taught children the value of hard work and claimed that many widows depended on the money their working children brought to their households. The bosses also said that their businesses would not survive without cheap child labor. Despite the business owners' protests, child labor was finally banned in 1938.

Addams realized that she could not help all the poor people in America by herself. She could see that poverty would be an ongoing problem unless the laws were changed.

She began to talk with politicians at the state capital in Springfield, Illinois, trying to persuade them to improve the laws about child labor, factory conditions, and the justice system for young people. Addams worked to limit women's work hours to eight hours a day and to make school free and compulsory for all children.

Changes didn't happen overnight, but people began to listen to Addams. Other citizens started to speak out against child labor, and attitudes began to change. Gradually, the laws were reformed.

Addams knew that it was necessary to change people's attitudes in order to bring about positive changes in society. In addition to working to improve the lives and rights of individuals, she also worked to help groups of people who were treated unfairly because of their race. She co-founded the American Civil Liberties Union (ACLU) and the National Association for the Advancement of Colored People (NAACP). Both of these organizations still exist today and continue to fight for the rights of all individuals.

A Responsibility to Change Things For the Better

Addams believed that everyone has a responsibility to help others and to work to bring about positive changes in society. Throughout her life, she was passionate about bringing about change. She was an advocate for ethnic minorities; she worked to improve health services for children and the poor; and she worked to promote peace. She wrote: "What after all has maintained the human race on this old globe, despite all the calamities of nature and all the tragic failings of mankind, if not the faith in new possibilities and the courage to advocate them?"

Addams also tried to change the way people thought about war. She felt that war was wrong, and she tried to stop World War I by speaking out against it. Addams traveled around giving speeches against the war. Many people supported her efforts, and she helped found a number of organizations to promote peace, including the Women's Peace Party and the International Congress of Women. Addams also became the first president of the Women's International League for Peace and Freedom.

The Women's Peace Party delegates sailed on this ship to the International Congress of Women in the Hague in 1915.

Not everyone supported Addams' efforts. Her pacifism made her very unpopular with some people—she received nasty letters and some newspapers wrote disapproving things about her—but Addams was determined and focused. She never stopped doing what she thought was right. Perhaps she couldn't stop World War I, but she knew that she was entitled to speak her mind, and she never gave up trying to change people's attitudes about war.

Jane Addams is one of America's best-loved and most well-respected leaders. She spent her life striving for positive change for all people, regardless of age, race or gender, until her death in 1935.

Addams was courageous and determined. Although she had frequent periods of illness throughout her life, she refused to let this stand between her and her goals of improving the lives of the disadvantaged. In 1931, Addams received the Nobel Peace Prize in recognition of her life's work. This award acknowledged the importance of her contribution to the world.

Addams was the first American woman to receive the Nobel Peace Prize.

Time Line: Jane Addams	
1860	born, Cedarville, IL
1881	graduates from Rockford Female Seminary
1887	visits Toynbee Hall
1889	founds Hull House
1909	helps found NAACP
1910	publishes *Twenty Years at Hull House*
1915	helps found the Women's Peace Party and organizes the International Congress of Women
1919	helps found the Women's International League for Peace and Freedom
1920	helps found the American Civil Liberties Union
1931	receives the Nobel Peace Prize
1935	dies, Chicago, IL

Respond to Reading

Summarize

Use important details from *Jane Addams: A Woman of Action* to summarize what you learned about Addams. Your graphic organizer may help you.

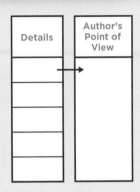

Details	Author's Point of View
→	

Text Evidence

1. What type of text is *Jane Addams: A Woman of Action*? How do you know this? **GENRE**

2. What does the author think about Jane Addams? Give details the author uses that reflect her point of view. **AUTHOR'S POINT OF VIEW**

3. The word *illness* on page 4 includes the suffix *-ness*. The suffix *-ness* means "the state of." Use the meaning of *-ness* and context clues to help you define the word *illness*. Identify a prefix or suffix in the word *autobiography* on page 9. **PREFIXES AND SUFFIXES**

4. Write about the author's view of Addams's work to have child labor banned and to help women, the impoverished, and ethnic minorities. Look for details in the text that support your answer. **WRITE ABOUT READING**

Compare Texts
Read about an individual who worked to make positive changes for Mexican Americans.

Gus García
Takes on Texas

It was 1950 in Jackson County, East Texas, and a man named Pete Hernández had just been arrested. Hernández's mother asked the lawyer, Gustavo C. García (known as Gus), to defend her son.

García was a Mexican American who had a burning desire to end racial discrimination in America. As part of this goal, he wanted to ensure that all people received a fair trial.

Even though the law said that anyone could be on a jury, in reality, Mexican Americans, African Americans, and women were never selected for juries. This meant that Hernández would surely have an all-white jury. García felt a jury that was so different from the **defendant** would find it difficult to remain neutral when listening to Hernández's case.

Gus García was a civil rights lawyer in East Texas.

Library of Congress, Prints & Photographs Division, NYWT&S Collection, [LC-USZ62-137627]

García jumped at the opportunity defend Hernández. He thought he could use this case to help change the **judicial system**. He asked other lawyers to help him. At Hernández's trial in 1951, García raised an objection, stating that the trial was unfair because there weren't any Mexican Americans on the jury.

The judge argued that Hispanic people could be on juries, and that it was just chance that there were no Hispanic people on this jury. However, García and his team of lawyers had done their research in anticipation that the judge would say this. They told the court that no one with a Hispanic last name had ever been on a jury in Jackson County

The judge overruled the lawyers, and Hernández was sentenced to life imprisonment. García appealed to another court. The second court turned down his appeal.

García had one more chance to appeal. He could ask the United States Supreme Court to hear his complaint. This was a risky and expensive thing to do. If García and his team won, it would make a positive change to the lives of their people. However, if they lost, it would strengthen the idea that Mexican Americans could be treated as second-class citizens.

By now, all Texans knew about these brave lawyers. Poor Hispanic people raised money to help pay the costs of the case. García's team submitted their appeal to the highest court in the land. The Supreme Court agreed to hear the appeal, and in 1954, the lawyers appeared in front of the Justices. This court had never made a decision about the rights of Mexican Americans before. García spoke so powerfully that the Justices were riveted.

The Supreme Court building is in Washington D.C.

Four months later, the United States Supreme Court announced its decision. Hernández would be tried again. This time, he would be tried before a jury that included Mexican Americans and people from other previously excluded groups.

Gus García and his team had made history. Defendants were now more likely to have a neutral jury. This was also a victory for not only Hispanics, but for all citizens of the United States of America because it ensured that everyone could be part of the judicial process.

Endnote: At his second trial Pete Hernández was again found guilty.

Ed Clark/Time & Life Pictures/Getty Images

Make Connections

Why was García so concerned about changing the jury system in Texas? **ESSENTIAL QUESTION**

What personal qualities did Jane Addams and Gus García both have? **TEXT TO TEXT**

Glossary

advocate *(AD-vuh-kuht)* someone who supports or promotes the interests of someone else *(page 9)*

defendant *(di-FEN-duhnt)* the person who is being accused in court *(page 16)*

economic gap *(e-kuh-NAH-mik gap)* the difference between the incomes of the rich and the poor *(page 6)*

emulated *(EM-yew-lay-tud)* trying to be like someone you admire *(page 3)*

expansive *(ik-SPAN-siv)* spreading out to considerable extent, broad *(page 6)*

judicial system *(jew-DI-shuhl SIS-tuhm)* the courts and the branch of government that enforces laws *(page 17)*

philanthropist *(fuh-LAN-thruh-pist)* a person who cares about humankind and does kind and charitable deeds *(page 2)*

Index

Focus on
Social Studies

Purpose To understand how changes in the past have made a difference to our lives today

What to Do

Step 1 With a small group, discuss what life would be like if you lived 100 years ago and had to work in a factory every day. Use the text and other sources for information.

Step 2 Make a two-column chart on a piece of paper. Label one column "100 Years Ago." Then write an imaginary daily schedule for your day 100 years ago. Don't forget that your day would possibly begin before sunrise.

Step 3 Label the second column "Today" and write your typical daily schedule. Include the things you learn at school, the things you do after school, and your evening routines.

Step 4 Discuss the two schedules with your group, noting the things that are the same and the things that are different. Write about the similarities and differences in the two schedules. Which schedule do you like better? Why?